From the Au

Love, Unity, Sex & Trust

L.U.S.T.! in Marriage

To Husbands; Wives and Engaged Couples:

As God's chosen ones, holy and beloved, clothe yourselves with compassion, kindness, humility, meekness, and patience. Bear with one another and, if anyone has a complaint against another, forgive each other; just as the Lord has forgiven you, so you also must forgive. Above all, clothe yourselves with love, which binds everything together in perfect harmony. And let the peace of Christ rule in your hearts, to which indeed you were called in the one body. And be thankful. Let the word of Christ dwell in you richly; teach and admonish one another in all wisdom; and with gratitude in your hearts sing psalms, hymns, and spiritual songs to God. And whatever you do, in word or deed, do everything in the name of the Lord Jesus, giving thanks to God the Father through him. Colossians 3:12-17 (NRSV)

A <u>*Beyond*</u> Good Marriage Requires:
Love, Unity, Sex and Trust *(Faith)*!

Reverends Steve & Bev

xulon
PRESS

Copyright © 2011 by Reverends Steve & Bev

L.U.S.T.!!!
Love, Unity, Sex and Trust in Marriage
by Reverends Steve & Bev

Printed in the United States of America

ISBN 9781612156293

All rights reserved solely by the author. The author guarantees all contents are original and do not infringe upon the legal rights of any other person or work. No part of this book may be reproduced in any form without the permission of the author. The views expressed in this book are not necessarily those of the publisher.

Unless otherwise indicated, Bible quotations are taken from THE HOLY BIBLE, NEW INTERNATIONAL VERSION®, NIV®. Copyright © 1973, 1978, 1984, 2010 by Biblica, Inc™.

www.xulonpress.com

About the Book and the Authors

"L.U.S.T.! in Marriage" is a must read! It should be used as a guide for developing successful marriages. God has used this couple to write a book that is inspired by the Word of God, yet presented in a manner that is straight forward and a delight to read. Reverend Steve and Reverend Bev use a tinge of humor and common sense to address issues that are destroying secular and Christian marriages.

The format of "L.U.S.T." is unique. The book consist of quotes from the famous and infamous, scriptures of strength, biblical teachings, and marital stories blended together to provide real life solutions to real life marital challenges.

I recommend the material in this book to those seeking to bring passion into their marriage or those desiring to conduct marriage seminars and workshops.

Dr. David Carter

Acknowledgements

***T**o God Be the Glory!* We would like to first thank the Lord Jesus Christ for giving us the revelation of what to share with couples and our call to work on His behalf to enrich marriages. We thank Jesus for every experience which He has exposed us to in life and in our ministry. It is those experiences that we are blessed to share with you through "L.U.S.T.! in Marriage".

Rev. Dr. Anthony Mays:
> Who ordained us, nurtured us, and provided us an opportunity to minister over the radio and internet.

Our Dear Sons & Friends:
> Thank you for your encouragement, support, proofreading skills, prayers, fasting, and so much love

Whosoever Will Christian Church:
> Pastor; Dr. Silvanus Bent, who mentored us and provided us with an opportunity serve as a couple on the church staff. To Pastor Edwin Lloyd and congregation who spoke life over our ministry.

Fort Washington Christian Church:
> Pastor Joseph Clark, Reverend Moses Blackmun, ministerial staff, Sunday School, Bible Study, Prayer Warriors, & congregation for continual spiritual support and resources.

Prophets, Apostles, Pastors, Teachers & Men and Women of God:
> We would also like to thank all of the Pastors and churches who have trusted us in their

L.U.S.T.!!!

pulpits and who have allowed us to conduct workshops at their churches and conferences. Very special thanks to those who pray for us that we are unaware of!

Reverends Steve & Bev

L.U.S.T. in Marriage
(Love, Unity, Sex, and Trust)

L.U.S.T. Scripture: *But if we say we love God and don't love each other, we are liars. We cannot see God. So how can we love God, if we don't love the people we can see? 1 John 4:20 CEV*

Preface

Marriage is hard work! Especially when you consider you are bringing two people together who have different feelings, thoughts, and values to live together for the rest of their lives. Each person has baggage that they bring into a marriage. Baggage is bound to

L.U.S.T.!!!

cause conflict if a couple does not work to keep their marriage strong.

In the early stages of marriage; life together is serene. Everything is fine and dandy and sweeter than candy. However, as marriage and couples mature, calm seas become tossed and stormy oceans. The <u>lust</u> that brought them together sometimes appears to have departed. But, what God has put together can withstand any storm.

Fifty percent of all Christian and secular marriages end in divorce, which makes it even more important to learn how to keep the <u>L.U.S.T.</u> in marriage. Conflict that leads to divorce does not have to happen. Despite what secular experts say; couples can keep the excitement in marriages and regain the L.U.S.T. that was present when they made a decision to marry.

L.U.S.T. Scripture: *By night on my bed I sought him whom my soul loveth.*
- Song of Solomon

L.U.S.T.!!!

Let's be honest! Odds are when you first met your spouse you did not think about their parenting skills; you did not wonder if they were decent cooks, you did not wonder how high their SAT scores were. There was a physical or emotional attraction that made you yearn for them. Lust is a desire that is switched on by an exterior impression that we have of a person that turn on thoughts of selfish passion.

L.U.S.T Quote: *I love that you get cold when it is 71 degrees out. I love that it takes you an hour and a half to order a sandwich. I love that you get a little crinkle in your nose when you're looking at me like I'm nuts. I love that after I spend a day with you, I can still smell your perfume on my clothes. And I love that you are the last person I want to talk to before I go to sleep at night. And it's not because I'm lonely, and it's not because*

> *it's New Year's Eve. I came here tonight because when you realize you want to spend the rest of your life with somebody, you want the rest of your life to start as soon as possible.*
> *– When Harry Met Sally*

What you felt when you first met Harry or Sally was not love; it was lust! But with God's nurturing lust can transform into L.U.S.T.!

Secular Definition of Lust: Lust is:
1. To have an eager, passionate, and an especially obsessive desire and need for personal gratification or covetousness of a person or thing.
2. A Longing desire; eagerness to possess or enjoy
3. Extreme sexual desire

Definition of Love:
1. A profoundly tender, passionate affection for another person.
2. A feeling of warm personal attachment or deep affection, as for a lover, parent, child, or friend.
3. A sexual passion or desire.

Spiritual Definition of L.U.S.T.:
1. L = *Love* – Godly love for a spouse. Agape love for a spouse that surpasses all carnal understanding and withstands physical or financial challenges
2. U = *Unity* – The state or quality of being one; in mind and spirit with a spouse; in oneness. Bound together by the Holy Spirit.
3. S = *Sex* – To increase the desire to be intimate with one's spouse spir-

itually and physically. The intimacy includes physical intercourse; but also includes the melding of Love, Unity, and Trust into every aspect of marriage.
4. T = Trust – A firm reliance on the integrity, ability, or character of a spouse to stand on the Word of God regardless of temptations or external influences

The guidance within the pages of *"L.U.S.T. in Marriage"* will assist in putting the Love, Unity, Sex, and Trust back into your marriage.

Chapter 1

Love

Love Quote: *"I am my beloved, and my beloved is me." Song of Solomon*

Love and Marriage

Marriage separates humans from animals. Marriage provides structure and binds two separate souls into one. Marriage provides the structure that gives youth balance in a world of inconsistencies. Marriage brings families' together, cultures together, religions together and the nation together. Marriage merges two separate lives into one.

L.U.S.T.!!!

Love Scripture: *Enjoy life with your wife (spouse), whom you love, all the days of this meaningless life that God has given you under the sun- all your meaningless days. For this is your lot in life and in your toilsome labor under the sun. Ecclesiastes 9:9*

There are four types of "love" required for marriage: Agape, Phileo, Storge, and Eros. Each has a special role in developing L.U.S.T.

Agape - Agape love is an unconditional love. Agape love makes you desire to be around someone that you don't like. Agape loves take over when the other loves have been exhausted. This is a love that only the love of Jesus can provide. It is received through salvation. This love is demonstrated in Ephesians 5:25 when God (through the apostle Paul) demands husbands to love wives as Christ loved the church.

Phileo – Phileo is affection. It is the type love that good friendships are based on. Phileo love is easier to walk away from. Phileo love is the "joy" that comes from being around another. It is the Lord's desire that the husband and wife enjoy the tenderness that comes from the physical love of each other while they work through the deficiencies and imperfections that we all have.

Storge - Storge is an open display of affection with a motive attached to it. This love can result in a smack on the butt, a squeeze, or another public show of affection. Typically it is the wife that requires open affection. Men tend to think that women are mind readers, but a woman has to "feel" a touch or a hug.

Eros – Eros is bringing two bodies into a union. It's is more than intercourse. It is a blending of emotions and spirit. It is required to complete the union between husband and wife.

Love Scripture: *That's why a man leaves his father and mother and gets married. He becomes like one person with his wife. Matthew 19:5 CEV*

All of these components of love must be present in marriage and must be protected with all of the wisdom and strength that we can muster. A lack in any of these areas of love will deteriorate a marriage.

Love is a deep, tender, feeling of affection toward a person. It comes from a conscious acceptance of the faults, failures, and fortunes of the person. Love is manifested through the sense of oneness that comes from thinking about someone or by being in their presence. Often with love comes a feeling of intense desire and attraction toward a person with a strong desire for sex and romance.

Love Scripture: *Above all, love each other deeply, because love covers over a multitude of sins. 1 Peter 4:8 NIV*

L.U.S.T.!!!

Despite what the local palm reader may tell you, no one is a mind reader. You cannot assume that your spouse know that you love them. Show the love, show the unity, show the sexual desire, and show the trust that you have for your mate by using the simple tips that we have provided in *"L.U.S.T.! and Marriage"*.

Love Quote: *Love the heart that hurts you, but never hurt the heart that loves you.*

Tips to Keep Love in "L." U.S.T.

Love Scripture: *Behold, thou art fair, my love; behold, thou art fair; thou hast doves' eyes within thy locks: thy hair is as a flock of goats that appear from mount Gilead. Thy teeth are like a flock of sheep that are even shorn, which came up from the washing; whereof every one bear twins, and none is barren among them. Thy lips are like a thread of scarlet, and thy speech is comely: thy temples are like a piece of a pomegranate within thy locks. Thy neck is like the tower of David builded for an armoury, whereon there hang a thousand bucklers, all shields of mighty men. Thy two breasts are like two young roes that are twins, which feed among the lilies. Song of Solomon 4:1-5*

1. ***Life Time Commitment*** – On your wedding day the preacher said; "till death do you part"! You have chosen each other before God to stay together for a life time. You must be committed to stay with your spouse until one of you is laid to rest. A lifetime commitment means that you will not stray from or break the promises that you made to God.
2. ***Look at Your Spouse*** – Keep your eyes from wondering and checking out others. God made your spouse especially for you with all of their faults and shortcomings! See your spouse as a super star. See the positive attributes of your spouse. Yes your spouse is annoying sometimes, but you are too! Make a list of all of the things that attracted you to your spouse. Meditate on the list. Now praise God for giving you the mate that is perfect; for you!
3. ***Look In the Mirror and Change that Person*** – Change how you react to problems. Before you

L.U.S.T.!!!

---

blame your spouse or try to change your spouse; ask yourself, what actions you could have taken to have avoided or improved a situation? Most adults don't drastically change, so your best bet is to accept your spouse and love them as they are.

Love Quote: *Jon Bon Jovi said; "It's easy to say, 'I love you,' to someone, but it's more meaningful to thank someone for loving you."*

4. Let Go of Pride – You do not always have to win or have your way. Do not allow your pride to get in the way of loving your spouse. Remember you and your spouse are not competitors; but team mates with the same goals and purpose.

Love Scripture: *Pride goeth before destruction, and an haughty spirit before a fall. Proverbs 16:18*

5. ***Learn Your Spouse*** – Do you know what your spouse likes? What they dislike? If not, watch, learn, and ask questions. When you know each other, do the things for each other that you know are special. If you practice treating your spouse, the way you want to be treated, amazing things will happen.
6. ***Launch an Improved Love Life*** – Love is more than sex. Have a date night, at least once or twice a month. Do the unexpected in and outside of the bedroom. Think outside of the box and make life an adventure again. Go on a new journey! Then seal the night in a "very" special way!

Love Quote: *"You come to love not by finding the perfect person, but by seeing an imperfect person perfectly." – Sam Keen*

7. ***Let Go of Resentment*** – Address issues immediately. Never let problems or concerns grow without being addressed. If some action

L.U.S.T.!!!

has worked your last nerve, say so. The worst thing that you can do is allow resentment for your spouse to build inside of you. Resentment wears you down and will eventually destroy the love that you have for beloved.

8. *Laugh Together* – Don't be too serious all of the time! Make an effort to have fun. Go see romantic comedy. Check out a comedy club. Laugh at each other's quirks and idiosyncrasies. Everything does not have to be about work, the kids, finances, or the mundane things of the marriage. Find humor in the midst of dread. And remember to always stay positive.

Love Quote: Maybe God put a few bad people in your life, so when the right one came along you'd be thankful. - Andrea Kiefer

9. *Little Things Mean a Lot* – It is important to avoid even the appearance of taking your loved one for granted. When we were

children our parents taught us to say, thank you, please, and to be grateful for just about anything that anyone did for us! It is important that we ensure that our mate knows that we recognize and appreciate "EVERYTHING" that they do for us. Just don't criticize the bad; but acknowledge the good.

10. *Long Lasting Relationship* – Forgiveness, patience, and love are three of the most important traits to have in a marriage. Forgiveness means that if your spouse makes a mistake that you will still love them. You may be upset with them for a moment, but forgive them anyway! No one is perfect including you! You both will make mistakes.

Love Scripture: *Love suffers long and is kind; love does not envy; love does not parade itself, is not puffed up; does not behave rudely, does not seek its own, is not pro-*

voked, thinks no evil; does not rejoice in iniquity, but rejoices in the truth; bears all things, believes all things, hopes all things, endures all things. Love never fails. 1 Corinthians 13:4-8

Biblical Couple that Illustrates Love in Marriage

Adam and Eve

After God made Adam in His image, God gave Adam a wife, Eve. Eve was the perfect gift. In the beginning this couple was complete and confident. They both were young, innocent, and in tune with God. They were transparent before each other and they both trusted God. As time went by, one of the couple was influenced by a relationship outside of the marriage. Both Adam and Eve were forced to leave their home because:

1. They forgot that they were the image of God
2. They forgot all God had done for them
3. They did not consult God before they made decisions
4. They listened to ungodly advice
5. They blamed others for their bad decisions
6. They disobeyed the Word of God

L.U.S.T.!!!

God was angry with Adam and Eve, but He did not leave them unprotected! Before they were evicted from Eden, God supplied Adam and Eve with everything that they needed. As they went into the unknown God furnished them with clothing. This is the most important part of the story! God will keep His covenant with you and your spouse regardless what the two of you have done. You made a promise before God that you would stay with your spouse. So keep your promise.

Key Verses: Genesis 1:26-27, Genesis 3:9-13, Genesis 3:21

Love Quote: *Where there is love, there is God also. - Leo Tolstoy*

"Love Notes"

1. Love the Lord with All Thine Heart
2. Send Flowers to Your Spouse's Job
3. Reenact Your Wedding Night
4. Brush Your Spouse's Hair
5. Keep Compliments Flowing
6. Take a Moonlit Walk
7. Write a Love Poem
8. Say I Love You
9. Don't Nag

Chapter 2

Unity

Unity Quote: *Mahatma Gandi said, "For unity to be real it must stand the severest strain without breaking."*

Unity and Marriage

The earthly parents of Jesus serve as role models of a unified couple. They withstood trials in the midst of living for God. The attributes of Joseph are described in Matthew 1:18-25. He was a righteous man who obeyed the Lord. Matthew 1:19 describes Joseph as just, virtuous, and devoted. Matthew 1:20 says he was open to the revelation of the Lord. As a husband Joseph was protective and caring for his wife. He guided her through the dangers of the desert and provided for her.

Unity Scripture: *If you have any encouragement from being united with Christ, if any comfort from his love, if any fellowship with the Spirit, if any tenderness and compassion, then make my joy complete by being like-minded, having the same love, being one in spirit and purpose Philippians 2:1-2*

Mary serves as a role model for today's wives. Her attributes are described in Luke 1:38-56. In Luke 1:38 She speaks to the angel of the Lord and outwardly voice her commitment to the Lord; *"I am the handmaiden of the Lord; let it be to me according to your word."* Luke 1:47 Mary displays the attributes of a praise leader and prayer warrior. In verse 56 Mary shows her love and commitment to her family.

Unity Scripture: *A wife should put her husband first, as she does the Lord. A husband is the head of his wife, as Christ is the head and the Savior of the church, which is his own body. Wives should always put their husbands first, as the church puts Christ first. A husband should love his wife as much as Christ loved the church and gave his life for it. He made the church holy by the power of his word, and he made it pure by washing it with water. Christ did this, so that he would have a glorious and holy church, without faults or spots or wrinkles or any other flaws. In the same way, a husband should love his wife as much as he loves himself. A husband who loves his wife shows that he loves himself. None of* *us hate our own bodies. We provide for them and take good care of them, just as Christ does for the church, because we are each part of his body. Ephesians 5:22-30 CEV*

What God has united let no one pull asunder! When a couple is unified in their thoughts and actions they can overcome more than they can as individuals. Unity in marriage is a deep feeling of affection and trust in a spouse. It is developed through faith in knowing that you can depend on and trust your spouse to stand by you, during the best and worse times. This faith comes from having "oneness" in purpose and goals.

Unity Scripture: *If you fall, your friend can help you up. But if you fall without having a friend nearby, you are really in trouble. If you sleep alone, you won't have anyone to keep you warm on a cold night. Someone might be* *able to beat up one of you, but not both of you. As the saying goes, "A rope made from three strands of cord is hard to break." Ecclesiastes 4:10-12 CEV*

Unity Quote: *In union there is strength. Aesop*

Tips to Keep UNITY in L. *"U."* S.T.

Unity Quote: *When you make the sacrifice in marriage, you're sacrificing not to each other but to unity in a relationship – Joseph Campbell*

1. ***Unbind Your Passion*** **–** Do not withhold your body from your spouse because of a disagreement. Your body is not yours alone, but is meant to be shared with your spouse. Sex is very important in unifying a married couple. Even if you feel that the ties that bind you are loosening, sex can frequently restore your bond.

Unity Scripture: *And over all these virtues put on love, which binds them all together in perfect unity. Colossians 3:14 NIV*

2. ***Understand Yourself*** **–** You cannot hope to walk as one with your

spouse if you do not know who you are.

Unity Quote: *Even the weak become strong when they are united.*
- Johann Von Schiller

3. ***Unique Marriage*** – Each marriage is different. Your marriage is unique to you and your spouse. Your marriage will not be like your parents, the Huxtables, or the Simpsons! Make your own family traditions. The information in this book will greatly assist you; however, a lot of marriage is on the job training. You will learn through the years what works best for you. Implement your best practices.
4. ***Unafraid*** – God made your spouse especially for you. You may not be able to fully understand their quirks or habits; nevertheless trust God. Believe that the spouse that you have was custom built by God for you. Be confident that God has a plan for both of you that will be manifested through your spouse.

L.U.S.T.!!!

Unity Scripture: *But while he thought on these things, behold, the angel of the LORD appeared unto him in a dream, saying, Joseph, thou son of David, fear not to take unto thee Mary thy wife: for that which is conceived in her is of the Holy Ghost. Matthew 1:20*

5. ***Upright, Holy in Thoughts and Actions–*** Do not look for a secular fix to a spiritual problem. Regardless of the situations you may face, stay pure and righteous. Do the right thing as directed by the Word of God. Seek advice from saved counselors or family members. Be holy!

Unity Scripture: *"Finally, all of you should agree and have concern and love for each other. You should also be kind and humble." 1 Peter 3:8 CEV*

L.U.S.T.!!!

---

6. ***Unselfish in Deeds*** **-** Compromise is a part of marriage. You should always be open to suggestions, adjustments and welcome the opportunity to experience new things. Do the things that you know will help your marriage. Cook, pick up the kids, visit your in-laws and perform all those tasks that make your spouses' life easier. It will strengthen the marriage.

Unity Scripture: *And let us consider how we may spur one another on toward love and good deeds. Hebrews 10:24*

7. ***Understand How to Work Through Problems*** **-** You should learn from your past mistakes and move ahead. Life is too short to waste second guessing decisions. Don't spend undue time wondering about how things could have been or should have been. Concentrate on understanding how to fix or improve the present circumstance. Focus on what is about to take place.

L.U.S.T.!!!

---

8. ***Use the Volume Control Switch –*** Turn down the volume from outside sources. External noises can be friends, family, hobbies, habits or other external forces that fight for your time and attention. Remember to always put your spouse first! Listen to the Holy Spirit and what God says about you and your marriage.

Unity Quote: *Cultivate solitude and quiet and a few sincere friends, rather than mob merriment, noise and thousands of nodding acquaintances.*
- William Powell

9. ***Unemotional Arguments -*** Before you lose your temper; put yourself in time out. Attacking your mate and not addressing the issue is not going to help you to resolve an issue. Take a deep breath! Yelling, screaming, and breaking your belongings will not help the situation. You are just going to have to replace everything that you

L.U.S.T.!!!

destroyed during your temper tantrum. You must be in control during an argument. Words spoken in the heat of an argument cannot be taken back after you have cooled down. Count to ten, leave the room, seek professional help, do whatever it takes to keep your emotions out of an argument. The health of your marriage is at stake.

Unity Scripture: *Wherefore, my beloved brethren, let every man be swift to hear, slow to speak, slow to wrath: James 1:19 KJV*

10. ***Unimportant Things*** – Pick your battles. Argue over things worth arguing over. Married people sometimes complain over the most unimportant things. Sample nonsense topics: toilet seats, two-ply or single-ply tissue, toothpaste tops, paper on the sofa, etc. Fill in the blanks! Save your knock-out drag-out fights (with rules) for important matters.

11. ***Unleash the Past Hurt*** – Check your baggage! Previous relationships can affect a marriage. Couples who have been extremely hurt in past relationships often use the bad experiences to determine how they interact in new relationships. It is important that excess baggage be checked at the gate and not allowed to board with the new passenger (spouse). You have a new spouse. Don't allow the baggage from the past to destroy the unity that you wish to build in this marriage.

Unity Scripture: *Reckless words pierce like a sword, but the tongue of the wise brings healing. Proverbs 12:18*

12. ***Unified in Prayer and Worship*** – Pray more! Fast Often! Worship always! A couple has to stay on their knees in prayer. Prayer and fasting changes things! Pray for the Holy Spirit. He will assist you in being on one accord. Pray with

your spouse until the power of the Holy Spirit enters into your situation.

Biblical Couple that Illustrates Unity in Marriage

Zacharias and Elizabeth

THERE was in the days of Herod, the king of Judaea, a certain priest named Zacharias, of the course of Abia: and his wife was of the daughters of Aaron, and her name was Elisabeth. And they were both righteous before God, walking in all the commandments and ordinances of the Lord blameless. And they had no child, because that Elisabeth was barren, and they both were now well stricken in years. And it came to pass, that while he executed the priest's office before God in the order of his course, According to the custom of the priest's office, his lot was to burn incense when he went into the temple of the Lord. And the whole multitude of the people were praying without at the time of incense. And there appeared unto him an angel of the Lord standing on the right side of the altar of incense. And when Zacharias saw him, he was troubled, and fear fell upon him. But

L.U.S.T.!!!

the angel said unto him, Fear not, Zacharias: for thy prayer is heard; and thy wife Elisabeth shall bear thee a son, and thou shalt call his name John. And thou shalt have joy and gladness; and many shall rejoice at his birth. Luke 1:5-14 KJV

Both Zacharias and Elizabeth were righteous before the Lord. They worked in the church and were faithful servants. It was years before their prayers were answered. Nevertheless, they stayed on their knees until God blessed them with John the prophet. This couple had to be prepared for the blessing that God was sending their way. It took years of prayer and worship for this couple to be ready to be the parents of John a blessing from God.

God is preparing you and your spouse to be blessed beyond anything that you could imagine or hope for. Don't give up and don't lose faith.

Unity Scripture: *Now unto him that is able to do exceeding abundantly above all that we* *ask or think, according to the power that worketh in us, Unto him be glory in the church by Christ Jesus throughout all ages, world without end. Amen. Ephesians 3:20-21*

"Unity Notes"

1. Keep God First in Everything
2. Be Spouses' Number 1 Fan
3. Don't Compete with Your Spouse
4. Have Date Nights without the Kids
5. Include Spouse in Your Decisions
6. Say Sorry and Mean IT
7. Accept Your Differences
8. Share Hobbies
9. Fight Fairly

Chapter 3

Sex

Sex Quote: *"I know nothing about sex, because I was always married."*
- Zsa Zsa Gabor

Sex in Marriage

We find it interesting that in the movies the single couples are the ones that have plenty of enjoyable sex. However, when the married couples are shown they are shown in mundane situations without L.U.S.T. Wow; why? Sex in the lives of married people should be shown in a more positive light. Lovemaking as a married couple is legal and held in high regards by God! He made us to be fruitful and to multiply!

You cannot be fruitful if you are not planting seeds. We all are sinners. We all break a commandment or two on a regular basis. However, as a married couple the "be fruitful" command given by God is a command that should be easy to obey! And obeyed quite frequently!

Married church people get embarrassed when the topic of sex arises. Nevertheless, church youth still manage to get pregnant, adultery occurs in the church, and the people with their names on church roles have abortions.

Christian couples should take the time to research what the bible says about sex. Sex in the life of a Christian couple is one of the most misunderstood issues in the church. I have heard of couples that had great love sessions until they joined a church. Then due to misguided teachings the couple stopped engaging in love making sessions that they both had previously found enjoyable. Their sexual activity became less frequent. Eventually, one of the couple went outside of the marriage looking for the passion that diminished after they became active in church. An active church life should not eliminate an active sex life! Forsake not the fellowship of the spouse in favor of the fellowship at church!

Sex Quote: *I want to wait to have sex until I'm married. Britney Spears*

One expert stated that many Christian women feel guilty about making love to their husbands. There have been many man-made cultural and societal rules imposed upon the church in regards to sex over the years that have nothing to do with what God teaches regarding sex.

Christian couples need to have a complete understanding of what the Bible actually says about sex. If the bible does not condemn it then you can do it! Sex is necessary for a strong marriage, and beyond certain biblical taboos, Christian couples should feel free to decide what is best for them sexually.

Marriage should not mean the end to sexual intimacy. It is your responsibility to maintain your sexual health, to keep things interesting, and to make sure that you and your spouse are satisfied. When problems arise in your sex life, you should address the challenges and do what you can to improve your sex life.

It is common for sexuality to transform as your marriage matures. Usually the lust of newlyweds is replaced with the time constraints, work obligations and other stumbling blocks that come with marriage.

Sex Quote: *Sex is more than an act of pleasure, its' the ability to be able to feel so close to a person, so connected, so comfortable that it's almost breathtaking to the point you feel you can't take it. And at this moment you're a part of them. –Author Unknown*

Surveys indicate that men are interested in the frequency of sex while women are interested in the quality of sex. L.U.S.T. requires frequency and quality. Married couples are challenged to keep lovemaking fresh. Men are happy with familiarity. That's why a husband will wear the same outfit every Saturday. Women on the other hand love variety. We should break from the familiar in love making and be ready to introduce different approaches to stimulate enjoyable sex.

Sex Scripture: *Marriage is honourable in all, and the bed undefiled: but whoremongers and adulterers God will judge. Hebrews 13:4 KJV*

Couples in marriages that are not sexually active are at risk. Infidelity can be birth because of a lack of sexually intimacy. Make plans with your mate to actively promote your sex life. Each spouse is responsible for initiating love making sessions. Get the most from your sex life by openly and frequently discussing your desires with your spouse. Use your imagination to overcome physical challenges

Sex Quote: *Sex is emotion in motion.*
– Mae West

Remember the atmosphere for the best sex sessions is set before you enter the bedroom! It's the emotion that set sex

L.U.S.T.!!!

---

into motion! If you are married, you have been given heavenly permission to enjoy your spouse! Make love and do it often! It is an honorable act!

Tips to Keep Sex in L.U. "S". T.

Sex Quote: *Making love? It's a communion with a woman. The bed is the holy table. There I find passion — and purification. Omar Sharif*

1. ***Sexual Intimacy*** – You don't have to make love everyday; but it wouldn't hurt! Love making sessions a couple of times a week will strengthen many areas of your marriage. It has been said that a husband is a better communicator after sex and that a woman will have sex to communicate with her husband.
2. ***Spontaneous Combustion*** - Don't put out the spark! Where there is smoke there is fire. Sometimes you just can't wait until the time is right! If your spouse is ready to be intimate, set the roof on fire. Saying no to your spouse over and over again will put the flame out. Don't say no when the moment says yes.

L.U.S.T.!!!

Sex Scripture: *Then God blessed Noah and his sons, saying to them, "Be fruitful and increase in number and fill the earth. Genesis 9:1*

3. *Spoil Your Spouse* – Be the president of your spouses' fan club. You should spoil one another with tenderness. Give them breakfast in bed. Iron their clothes, give them compliments in the presence of others.

4. *Sensitivity* – Be sensitive to your loved one's feelings. Men and women react differently to circumstances. Nevertheless, we can anticipate how our spouse will react to certain actions or decisions we make. We should avoid doing things that we know will cause our spouse to be uncomfortable.

Sex Quote: *Marriage may often be a stormy lake, but celibacy is almost always a muddy horse pond – Thomas Love Peacock*

5. *Show Affection* – A pat on the butt in front of the kids can say more about your marriage than words could ever say. Whether it's a public kiss, a love note, or a smile when your loved one enters the room; happy couples are not afraid to publicly show affection.
6. *Share Your Thoughts* – What is on your mind when you are silent? It's important to communicate with your spouse. Share your thoughts, concerns and ideas with your loved one. Regularly sharing who you are becoming establishes an open environment for intimacy.
7. *Show Your Respect* - Be an advocate for your spouse! Sex can be improved when you have mutual respect for each others' desires. Additionally, respect outside of the bedroom creates a desire to be intimate. Stick up for them, support them, and never say anything bad about them to anybody!

L.U.S.T.!!!

Sex Scripture: *Let them be for yourself alone, and not for strangers with you.*

Let your fountain be blessed, and rejoice in the wife of your youth, a lovely deer, a graceful doe. Let her breasts fill you at all times with delight; be intoxicated always in her love. Why should you be intoxicated, my son, with a forbidden woman and embrace the bosom of an adulteress? For a man's ways are before the eyes of the LORD, *and he ponders all his paths. The iniquities of the wicked ensnare him, and he is held fast in the cords of his sin. He dies for lack of discipline, and because of his great folly he is led astray. Proverbs 5:17-23*

1. **Socialize with Each Other** – Your spouse should be your best friend. Limit girls' nights out and kicking it with the guys' night! Find things

that you like to do as a couple and do them. Have a date night and make your night a priority. Go to a movie, take in a play, get dressed up and go to a fancy restaurant. Be creative!

9. *Sensual and Saved* – Sensuality and saved is not an oxymoron! They go together like praise and worship. Let's talk to your saved side for a moment. We know that the Bible is the Word of God written by men guided by the Holy Spirit through revelation. We will assign you some homework. Read the Songs of Solomon. Ensure that you have a good concordance and commentary handy. God desired that the Song of Solomon be placed in the Bible for couples to know that God expects us to be intimate. Praise God for the new found liberty!

Sex Quote: *Two lives, two hearts joined together in friendship united forever in love. Anonymous*

L.U.S.T.!!!

---

10. ***Seeing is Believing*** – Avoid even the appearance of evil. Keep your eyes from wondering. Good sex requires that your spouse know that you see them as the one that you desire. If you are with your spouse and a beautiful person walks by keep your eyes on your mate.

11. ***Set the Atmosphere*** – Intimate moments together are special. Go out of your way to make sure that distractions are not preventing you from enjoying lovemaking. Turn off the phone, put the kids to bed early, turn the television off; get rid of the barriers that separate you from fully enjoying your spouse. We recommend that every couple of months you spend a weekend in an upscale hotel. Set the atmosphere with sexy sleep apparel, soft music, rose petals, sensual bath oils, chocolates, candles, and well you can take it from here! Use your imagination!

Love Quote: *Anyone can be passionate, but it takes real lovers to be silly.*
- Rose Franken

12. *Surprise Each Other* – Surprise your spouse by doing something that you have never done before. Foreplay begins before you get home from work. Send flowers to your spouses' office. Make a lunch appointment. Help with chores. Give each other massages. Do something different in the bedroom. Try out some Kama Sutra moves. Make sure that you both warm-up and stretch first!

13. *Satisfaction Guaranteed* – Tell your spouse what you desire. You would not go to an all you can eat restaurant and allow the waiter to pick your entree. Yet once you become married, you allow your spouse to pick what you are served. Discuss with your spouse the positions you prefer, what feels good, what does not feel good, your likes and your dislikes. There are plenty of satisfying

L.U.S.T.!!!

items on the menu. Make sure you place an order for what you want. By the way, it is okay for you to have your dessert before the main course!

Biblical Couple That Illustrates Sex in Marriage

King Solomon to His Wife

The Song of Solomon commends the virtues of marriage and the love between a husband and his wife. It is God's desire that a man and woman live together as a married couple. God desire that they love each other spiritually, emotionally, and physically. Enjoy these selected verses from the Song of Solomon.

Let him kiss me with the kisses of his mouth: for thy love is better than wine. Because of the savour of thy good ointments thy name is as ointment poured forth, therefore do the virgins love thee. Draw me, we will run after thee: the king hath brought me into his chambers: we will be glad and rejoice in thee, we will remember thy love more than wine: the upright love thee. Thy cheeks are comely with rows of jewels, thy neck with chains of gold. A bundle of myrrh is my well-beloved unto me; he shall lie all night betwixt my breasts. Behold, thou art fair, my love; behold, thou art fair; thou hast doves' eyes. Behold, thou art fair, my beloved, yea, pleasant: also our bed is green. By night on my bed I sought him whom my soul loveth: I sought him, but I found him not. I will rise now, and go about the city in the streets, and in the broad ways I will seek him whom my soul loveth: I sought him, but I found him not. The watchmen that go about the city found me: to whom I said, Saw ye him whom my soul loveth? Song of Solomon

This poem is divided into three sections: courtship, the wedding, and the maturing marriage. The song begins before the wedding, as the bride longs to be with her betrothed. She looks forward to the intimacy of marriage, but is unsure that she will meet Solomon's expectations. The king praises his fiancée's beauty, and let her know that she is more than he ever dreamed of and more than he deserves. On their wedding night, King Solomon reaffirms her beauty. The wife willingly gives herself fully to her King! They seal the night in a session of passionate lovemaking.

Like many marriages the King and Queen experience valleys and peaks that are depicted in a dream the queen has. In her dream she and the King separate. While in the dream, she searches for her husband which she eventually finds. The story ends with the married lovers being reunited and as happy as they were before the separation. They sing of love. They sing of their commitment. They sing of their need to be with each other!

Marriage is not in vogue anymore. Living together or divorce is seen as the normal way to do things. Some are even trying to redefine marriage. Solomon was wise to leave us with a song that encourages praising our spouse, encouraging our spouse, and loving our spouse.

The Apostle Paul said the following about marriage: *But because of the temptation to sexual immorality, each man should have his own wife and each woman her own husband. The husband should give to his wife her conjugal rights, and likewise the wife to her husband. For the wife does not have authority over her own body, but the husband does. Likewise the husband does not have authority over his own body, but the wife does. Do not deprive one another, except perhaps by agreement for a limited time, that* *you may devote yourselves to prayer; but then come together again, so that Satan may not tempt you because of your lack of self-control."* I Corinthians 7:2-5

"Sex Notes"

1. The Bedroom is Undefiled & Holy
2. Begin Each Day with a Kiss & Kindness
3. Use Best Practices & Lessons Learned
4. Backrubs & Massages are Great
5. Don't Neglect Your Appearance
6. Set Aside Time for Sex
7. Women Desire Quality
8. Men Quantity
9. All Desire Variety

Chapter 4

Trust

Trust Quote: *You may be deceived if you trust too much, but you will live in torment if you don't trust enough. – Frank Crane*

Trust in Marriage

We cannot depend on our limited understanding to know what to do to develop and improve our marriages. Our every action should be directed by biblical principles and guidance. Marriage counselors and relationship specialist are guided by theory and feelings. The Word is not theory. The Word works! Trust God and work the Word!

Trust Scripture: *For the man who does not love his wife but divorces her, says the Lord, the God of Israel, covers his garment with violence, says the Lord of hosts. So guard yourselves in your spirit, and do not be faithless. Malachi 2:16*

In marriage trust must is earned and developed over time. Most couples will marry because they have reached a level of trust that has allowed them to be able to share dreams, desires, and passion. There is no magic bottle that you can rub to gain the trust of a spouse, but it can be easily shattered by one indiscretion or slip of the tongue. Trust is required to maintain L.U.S.T in marriage. Trust is created by an open and honest relationship. Trust is obtained when your spouse is certain that you are their biggest supporter. Trust building should be a priority. Trust is a proactive measure that will prevent issues from becoming problems.

Trust Quote: *The only way to make a man trustworthy is to trust him.*
- Henry L. Stimson

Trust is required for a marriage to last. Without trust you will be miserable. To develop a relationship that will withstand the rough times that all marriages will have requires faith in God and faith in your spouse. A lack of faith in either hinders the ability to overcome adversity.

Doubting the ability of your spouse to trust you or doubting your ability to trust your spouse will affect every aspect of your life. Your work, your social life, your church life, and home life are affected when you lose trust in your mate. Trust is not automatic. It's something that a spouse earns.

Trust Quote: *"Trust is like a vase . . . .once it's broken, though you can fix it, the vase will never be the same." Author Unknown*

Trust is fragile. We should take precaution not to jeopardize the trust that our husband or wife has in us. Trust requires honesty, open communication, and unfailing love. Lastly, but most importantly, trust requires faith and the love that can only come through a relationship with Jesus.

Trust Scripture: *Trust in the LORD with all thine heart; and lean not unto thine own understanding. In all thy ways acknowledge him, and he shall direct thy paths. Proverbs 3:5-6 Kings James*

Trust in the Lord, don't stop loving, and take comfort in your salvation. Jesus will renew your heart and he will reestablish everything that you thought was taken.

L.U.S.T.!!!

Tips to Keep Trust in L.U.S. "T"

Trust Quote: We're never so vulnerable than when we trust someone - but paradoxically, if we cannot trust, neither can we find love or joy.
- Walter Anderson

1. ***Timeout On Acting Single*** *–* There is someone at home waiting for you. As a married couple you have new roles and responsibilities. You cannot party or stay out all night with friends. It's hard for a spouse to trust their lover when they are maintaining a single life style.

Trust Quote: The only one thing I can change is myself, but sometimes that makes all of the difference. – Anonymous

2. ***Time Together*** *–* Spend quality time with your spouse. If that means cutting out some of the outside activities that you have; do it. Your spouse is more important than

L.U.S.T.!!!

bowling or meeting with your college buddies. Try not to work late.

3. *Temptation* – Avoid the appearance of evil. Stay away from situations that put you at risk. Do not maintain on-going communication with old flames, do not go to lunch with the opposite sex, do not give inappropriate compliments, nor is it proper for you to flirt. Do not blame the Lord if you have taken yourself down a path that leads to temptation.

Trust Scripture: *Temptation comes from our own desires, which entice us and drag us away. James 1:14 NLT*

4. *Truthful* – Dishonestly births distrust! Be honest even if it makes you or your spouse uncomfortable. Trust comes by knowing that you and your mate are honest. If you do not want to do something do not lie and say that you will do it; when you have no intention of doing it.

L.U.S.T.!!!

5. *Talking* - You should talk about everything! Communicate, communicate and communicate. A successful marriage requires non-stop communication. Ensure that you talk about children, finances, family, work, and strategies for developing the family.

Trust Scripture: *Let the words of my mouth, and the meditation of my heart, be acceptable in thy sight, O LORD, my strength, and my redeemer Psalms 19:14 KJV*

6. *Touch Base* – Maintain contact with your mate. Be home or wherever you are suppose to be at the time that you tell your spouse you will be there. You cannot be missing in action for hours and expect to maintain a relationship of trust!
7. *Terminate Secrets* - You are not 007. Your marriage should be built on openness. Inform your spouse of any mistake or actions that you have taken that could affect the

marriage. Additionally, do not work with family members to develop activities or resolutions that your spouse does not know about. Admit mistakes, apologize, and explain how you will work to avoid repeating the mistake.

Trust Scripture: *And the rib, which the LORD God had taken from man, made he a woman, and brought her unto the man. And Adam said, This is now bone of my bones, and flesh of my flesh: she shall be called Woman, because she was taken out of Man. Genesis 2: 23 KJV*

8. *Threesomes Don't Work* – Keep others out of your relationship. Old flames should be put out! It is disrespectful to maintain "very close" ties with someone that was a past lover. Phone calls and harmless contact with former love interests

L.U.S.T.!!!

---

is setting the stage for a potential act of adultery.

9. ***Think Before You Speak*** - Remember whatever you say may be used against you. Everyone does not need to know what goes on in your home. There is a commercial that says what happens in Vegas stays in Vegas. We recommend that unless you are speaking to a marriage counselor that you do not share issues that you and your spouse are having within your marriage with anyone. We have seen cases where a "friend" or "confidant" uses sensitive information to seduce a spouse to participate in act of infidelity. Additionally, advice that you receive from a friend is based on their history and their relationships. Their fixes may not be the answer to what is broken in your marriage. Secular friends provide secular advice. Seek counseling from a spirit filled trained counselor. Seek Jesus!

Trust Scripture: *Death and life are in the power of the tongue, and they who indulge in it shall eat the fruit of it [for death or life]. Proverbs 18:21 AMP*

10. Tear Down Walls – Let your spouse inside your fortress! You can be transparent with your lover. Allow your spouse to enter pass the walls that you have established. Sometimes the hurts of our past causes us to place emotions, dreams, and who we really are behind walls. Believe me your spouse knows when you are hiding something. Trust and love grow through vulnerability. Let your spouse love you for who you are.

Trust Quote: *I have had more trouble with myself than with any other man I've met. – Dwight Moody*

11. *Teamwork* – You and your spouse are a team. You should have one heart, one mind, and one purpose. God is the owner of the team, Jesus in the coach, and the Holy Spirit is the quarterback. As a player on the team you do not make any decisions without getting approval from the leadership. Teamwork makes the dream work!
12. *Try Asking for Forgiveness* – Trust is built over time. It may take time to re-establish trust in a relationship that has trust issues. Forgiving someone who has violated a trust requires that the violator asks for forgiveness and be willing to take the punishment. Sometimes it's not enough to say you're sorry. Often it requires showing a change in habits and an improvement in character.

Trust Scripture: *If we confess our sins, he is faithful and just to forgive us our sins and to cleanse* *us from all unrighteousness. 1 John 1:9 KJV*

13. *Try to Forgive* - Forgive, let go and move forward with your life. Your spouse loves you and did not intentionally try to damage you. Forgive them. They do love you. Forgiveness is the best way to learn to trust again. Remember Christ forgave us for a multitude of sins.

Trust Scripture: *But I trust in your unfailing love; my heart rejoices in your salvation. Psalm 13:5 KJV*

Biblical Couple that Illustrates Trust in Marriage

Moses and Zipporah

Moses was a fugitive from Egypt. During his exile he came upon the seven daughters of Jethro at a well in the desert where they were watering their fathers' sheep. At the oasis, Moses battled men who harassed the girls. The father of the young women, Jethro, gives Moses his daughter Zipporah in marriage. Despite their religious and racial differences Moses and Zipporah become a happy unified couple. The marriage gives them two sons, Gershom and Eliezer.

Well into their marriage God speaks to Moses through a burning bush. After hearing from God Moses tells Zipporah that he must go back to Egypt to free his people form Pharaoh. Moses, Zipporah and their family return to Egypt to free the Hebrews from slavery.

Trust was showed by Zipporah. She married a man that was running from the law. He did not have any money; nor decent credit. But she could see the potential in him. She was from a close knit family, but she was willing to follow him into a desert and the possibility of death so that he could reach his destiny.

Why did Zipporah trust Moses with all of the baggage that he had?

1. Zipporah loved Moses
2. Moses was her hero
3. Moses was a her provider
4. Moses accepted Zipporah
5. Moses accepted Zipporah's family
6. Zipporah knew that Moses talked to God

Key Verses Exodus 2:18–20, Exodus 4:24-27

Trust Scripture: *This is how we know what love is: Jesus Christ laid down his life for us. And we ought to lay down our lives for each other. 1 John 3:16*

"Trust Notes"

1. Trust God! Not Your Own Understanding
2. Keep Lines of Communication Open
3. Admit That You Were Wrong
4. Have Realistic Expectations
5. Love & Respect Each Other
6. Think Before You Speak
7. Don't Maintain Secrets
8. Love and Respect Each Other
9. There Can Not Be Jealousy in Marriage
10. Honesty is Always the Best Policy

Conclusion

L.U.S.T. and Marriage

L.U.S.T. requires giving and sacrifice.

L.U.S.T is expressed by what we say.

L.U.S.T is expressed by what we do.

Put Love, Unity, Sex, and Trust (L.U.S.T.) back into your marriage! Remember what the Word of God says when you feel like giving up on your spouse and your marriage!

1. *God Desires That We Marry!*
   Then the LORD God said, "It is not good that the man should be alone; I will make him a helper as his partner." So out of the ground the LORD God

formed every animal of the field and every bird of the air, and brought them to the man to see what he would call them; and whatever the man called every living creature, that was its name. The man gave names to all cattle, and to the birds of the air, and to every animal of the field; but for the man there was not found a helper as his partner. So the LORD God caused a deep sleep to fall upon the man, and he slept; then he took one of his ribs and closed up its place with flesh. And the rib that the LORD God had taken from the man he made into a woman and brought her to the man. Then the man said, "This at last is bone of my bones and flesh of my flesh; this one shall be called Woman, for out of Man this one was taken." Therefore a man leaves his father and his mother and clings to his wife, and they become one flesh. Genesis 2:18-12 NRSV

2. ***Marriage Requires Sacrifice, Worship, and Transformation!***
   I appeal to you therefore, brothers and sisters, by the mercies of God, to

present your bodies as a living sacrifice, holy and acceptable to God, which is your spiritual worship. Do not be conformed to this world, but be transformed by the renewing of your minds, so that you may discern what is the will of God — what is good and acceptable and perfect. Let love be genuine; hate what is evil, hold fast to what is good; love one another with mutual affection; outdo one another in showing honor. Do not lag in zeal, be ardent in spirit, serve the Lord. Rejoice in hope, be patient in suffering, persevere in prayer. Romans 12: 1-1, 9-12 NRSV

3. Marriage Requires Submission to Christ-like Love!

And live in love, as Christ loved us and gave himself up for us, a fragrant offering and sacrifice to God. Be subject to one another out of reverence for Christ. Wives, be subject to your husbands as you are to the Lord. For the husband is the head of the wife just as Christ is the head of the church, the body of which he is the Savior. Just as the church is subject to Christ, so also wives ought to be, in everything, to their husbands. Husbands, love your wives, just as Christ loved the church and gave himself up for her, in order to make her holy by cleansing her with the washing of water by the word, so as to present the church to himself in splendor, without a spot or wrinkle or anything of the kind — yes, so that she may be holy and without blemish. In the same way, husbands should love their wives as they do their own bodies. He who loves his wife loves himself. For no one ever hates his own body, but he nourishes and tenderly cares for it, just as Christ does for the church, because we are members of his body. For this reason a man will leave his father and mother and be joined to his wife, and the two will become one flesh." This is a great mystery, and I am applying it to Christ and the church. Each of you, however, should love his wife as himself, and a wife should respect her husband. Ephesians 5:2a, 21-33 (NRSV)

4. Marriage Requires a Passion for Love, Peace, and Oneness!

As God's chosen ones, holy and beloved, clothe yourselves with compassion, kindness, humility, meekness, and patience. Bear with one another and, if anyone has a complaint against another, forgive each other; just as the Lord has forgiven you, so you also must forgive. Above all, clothe yourselves with love, which binds everything together in perfect harmony. And let the peace of Christ rule in your hearts, to which indeed you were called in the one body. And be thankful. Let the word of Christ dwell in you richly; teach and admonish one another in all wisdom; and with gratitude in your hearts sing psalms, hymns, and spiritual songs to God. And whatever you do, in word or deed, do everything in the name of the Lord Jesus, giving thanks to God the Father through him. Colossians 3:12-17 (NRSV)

5. *Marriage Requires Unity of Spirit, Godly Communication, and Righteousness!*
   Finally, all of you, have unity of spirit, sympathy, love for one another, a tender heart, and a humble mind. Do not repay evil for evil or abuse for abuse; but, on the contrary, repay with a blessing. It is for this that you were called — that you might inherit a blessing. For "Those who desire life and desire to see good days, let them keep their tongues from evil and their lips from speaking deceit; let them turn away from evil and do good; let them seek peace and pursue it. For the eyes of the Lord are on the righteous, and his ears are open to their prayer. 1 Peter 3:8-12a NRSV

6. *Marriage Requires Confidence in God and Prayer About Everything!*
   Don't worry about anything; instead, pray about everything; tell God your needs, and don't forget to thank Him for his answers. If you do this, you will experience God's peace, which is far more wonderful than the human

mind can understand. His peace will keep your thoughts and your hearts quiet and at rest as you trust in Christ Jesus. Philippians 4: 6-7 TLB

Benediction:

For I am convinced that nothing can ever separate us from His love. Death can't, and life can't. The angels won't, and all the powers of hell itself cannot keep God's love away. Our fears for today, or worries about tomorrow, or where we are — high above the sky, or in the deepest ocean — nothing will ever be able to separate us from the love of God demonstrated by our Lord Jesus Christ when he died for us. *Romans 8: 38-39 TLB*

Now Go and Get Your L.U.S.T Back!

Amen! Amen! Amen!

Contact Us at:
ReverendsSteveandBev@Yahoo.com
Facebook/ReverendsSteveandBev